# LONG ISLAND NATURE PRESERVES
## Coloring Book

### SY AND DOT BARLOWE

DOVER PUBLICATIONS, INC.
Mineola, New York

# ACKNOWLEDGMENTS

The publishers wish to thank the following for their cooperation in the creation of this book: 1, 30: U.S. Department of the Interior, National Park Service; 2, 3, 8, 10, 11, 15: Nassau County Department of Recreation & Parks, Division of Museums; 4: Town of North Hempstead, Department of Parks & Recreation; 5, 9: Town of Hempstead, Department of Conservation & Waterways; 6, 7: Old Westbury Gardens; 12: Planting Fields Foundation; 13: Theodore Roosevelt Sanctuary, Inc., National Audubon Society; 14: Town of Oyster Bay, Department of Parks; 16, 17: Cold Spring Harbor Fish Hatchery & Aquarium; 18, 19, 34, 35: U.S. Department of the Interior, Fish & Wildlife Service; 20, 31, 36, 37: The Nature Conservancy; 21, 26, 27, 28: New York State Office of Parks, Recreation & Historic Preservation; 22, 23: Town of Smithtown; 24, 25: Town of Islip, Department of Parks, Recreation & Cultural Affairs; 29: Marine Sciences Research Center, State University of New York at Stony Brook; 32, 33: Southampton Township Wildfowl Association; 38, 39: Riverhead Foundation for Marine Research and Preservation.

Published in Canada by General Publishing Company, Ltd., 30 Lesmill Road, Don Mills, Toronto, Ontario.
Published in the United Kingdom by Constable and Company, Ltd., 3 The Lanchesters, 162–164 Fulham Palace Road, London W6 9ER.

*Bibliographical Note*

*Long Island Nature Preserves Coloring Book* is a new work, first published by Dover Publications, Inc., in 1997.

DOVER *Pictorial Archive* SERIES

*International Standard Book Number: 0-486-29406-4*

Manufactured in the United States of America
Dover Publications, Inc., 31 East 2nd Street, Mineola, N.Y. 11501

# INTRODUCTION

Nearly 120 miles long and 23 miles across at its widest point, Long Island is a part of the Atlantic Coastal Plain. Unlike the remainder of the Coastal Plain, however, its terrain was modified by the advance and retreat of the Pleistocene glaciers. Of great interest geologically, it has the gently eastward sloping sedimentary strata and barrier islands typical of the Coastal Plain, as well as such glacial features as terminal moraines, outwash plains and kettle ponds.

Long Island is of just as much interest ecologically, for many endangered species—both plant and animal—make their home in the varied habitats to be found there. Whether your interest is in birds, mammals, fishes, insects, trees or plants, Long Island has much to offer.

There is a wide variety of parks, preserves, sanctuaries, gardens, arboretums, refuges and other organizations devoted to preserving wildlife on Long Island. It is impossible in a book of this size to present all of them, but the 27 featured in these pages provide a sampling of the natural wonders of Long Island protected for all time.

All of the sites are open to the public, although some have somewhat limited access. Wherever possible, hours of operation are listed, but since these are subject to change, please check before visiting. An address and telephone number has been included for each site; all telephone numbers are area code 516, with the exception of Jamaica Bay Wildlife Refuge, which is area code 718. The sites are presented roughly from the west to the east. A map showing the location of the sites can be found on the following pages.

The plants and animals shown are referred to by their common names with scientific names given in parentheses. Every effort has been made to use the most up-to-date nomenclature. Indexes of common and scientific names can be found on pages 40–41.

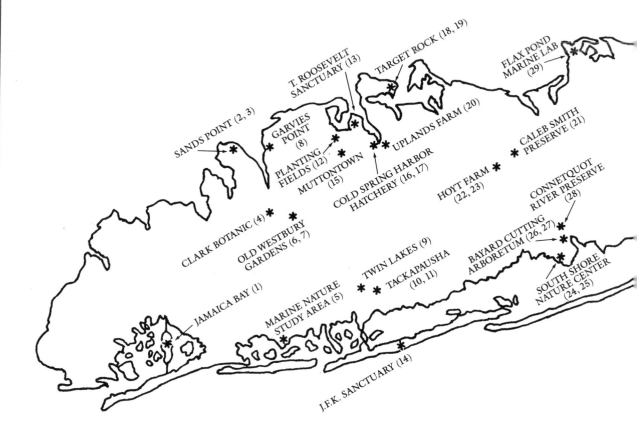

SANDS POINT (2, 3)

T. ROOSEVELT
SANCTUARY (13)

TARGET ROCK (18, 19)

FLAX POND
MARINE LAB
(29)

GARVIES
POINT
(8)

UPLANDS FARM (20)

CALEB SMITH
PRESERVE (21)

PLANTING
FIELDS (12)

MUTTONTOWN
(15)

COLD SPRING HARBOR
HATCHERY (16, 17)

HOYT FARM
(22, 23)

CONNETQUOT
RIVER PRESERVE
(28)

CLARK BOTANIC (4)

OLD WESTBURY
GARDENS (6, 7)

BAYARD CUTTING
ARBORETUM (26, 27)

TWIN LAKES (9)

TACKAPAUSHA
(10, 11)

SOUTH SHORE
NATURE CENTER
(24, 25)

JAMAICA BAY (1)

MARINE NATURE
STUDY AREA (5)

J.F.K. SANCTUARY (14)

Location of Preserves and Sanctuaries Included in This Volume
(the numbers are page numbers)

MASHOMACK
PRESERVE
(36, 37)

MONTAUK
(38/39)

RIVERHEAD
FOUNDATION
(38/39)

MORTON REFUGE
(34, 35)

MERRILL LAKE
(31)

QUOGUE REFUGE
(32, 33)

FIRE ISLAND
SEASHORE (30)

**Jamaica Bay Wildlife Refuge.** This 9000-acre wildlife refuge includes salt marshes, upland fields and woods, fresh and brackish water ponds and an open expanse of bay and islands. More than 325 species of birds have been recorded here. Address: Cross Bay Blvd. at Broad Channel, Queens, NY. Phone: (718) 318-4340. When to visit: trails open daily, sunrise to sunset. Required permit available at visitor's center (open 8:30 to 5).

The wading bird is a glossy ibis (*Plegadis falcinellus*); it is chestnut-colored with a green or purple gloss. The ducks with dotted white breasts are male common teal (*Anas crecca*); they have a gray body and a chestnut head with a green ear patch; behind them is a (mottled brown) gadwall (*Anas strepera*). At the right is a male long-tailed duck or oldsquaw (*Clangula hyemalis*) in summer plumage (white body and eye patch, black head and breast, dark brown back). The (yellow) flower in the left foreground is a Japanese honeysuckle (*Lonicera japonica*); at the right is a (pink) salt spray (or rugosa, or wrinkled) rose (*Rosa rugosa*).

1

**Sands Point Preserve.** Built in the early 1900s, this former estate of the Goulds and Guggenheims offers changing exhibits in palatial buildings and 216 acres of grounds, including self-guiding nature trails. It is operated by the Nassau County Department of Recreation & Parks. Address: 95 Middle Neck Road, Sands Point, NY 11050. Phone: 571-7900. When to visit nature trails: daily, 10 to 5.

The great horned owl (*Bubo virginianus*), brown with a white throat "bib," is seen nesting in an Eastern white pine (*Pinus strobus*).

**Sands Point Preserve** (*continued*). Visitors are admiring a 325-year-old black oak (*Quercus velutina*) in a forest setting. This oak species has a very dark bark. In the foreground is a mayapple (*Podophyllum peltatum*), which bears white flowers.

**Clark Botanic Garden.** This 12-acre living museum features three ponds, a canopy of white pine and hemlock, wooded areas and specialized gardens, including roses, herbs, wildflowers, dwarf conifers and rock plants, providing landscape and gardening ideas for home gardeners. A wide variety of horticultural and botanical programs is offered. Address: 193 I. U. Willets Road, Albertson, NY 11507-2298. Phone: 484-2208.

When to visit: Monday to Friday, 9 to 4:30, weekends, 10:30 to 4:30; closed winter weekends.

A bullfrog (*Rana catesbeiana*) sits on the pad of a (white) waterlily (*Nymphaea odorata*) in front of a clump of yellow flag (*Iris pseudacorus*). The frog is tawny with a greenish head and darker spots.

4

**Marine Nature Study Area.** Walking trails and eight instruction sites with visual aids were carefully planned so as not to disrupt the natural plant and animal communities on these 52 acres of the Hempstead estuary salt-marsh environment. Over 200 bird species have been recorded. An Interpretive Center offers marine life displays and saltwater aquaria featuring local species. Address: 500 Slice Drive, Oceanside, NY 11572.

Phone: 766-1580. When to visit: Tuesday to Saturday, 9 to 5; closed Sunday, Monday and holidays.

A snowy egret (*Egretta thula*)—a white bird with black bill and legs and yellow feet—towers over beach plants that include (right foreground) sea lavender (*Limonium* sp.) and (left) salt-meadow cord grass (*Spartina patens*).

**Old Westbury Gardens.** This replica of an 18th-century country estate includes a mansion and 70 acres of formal gardens, lawns, woods and small contemporary gardens to give ideas to home owners. Address: 71 Old Westbury Road, Old Westbury, NY 11568. Phone: 333-0048. When to visit: 10 to 5, Wednesday to Monday, May to December 15.

A tiger swallowtail (*Pterourus glaucus*), with its black-striped yellow wings, alights on a cultivated rose (*Rosa* sp.) alongside a garden walk.

**Old Westbury Gardens** (*continued*). On a wildflower walk:
purple trillium (*Trillium erectum*), with maroon or reddish-
brown blossoms, and, in the center, a jack-in-the-pulpit (*Aris-
aema triphyllum*), with its green or purplish-brown "hood."

**Garvies Point Museum and Preserve.** A museum of archaeology, Native American culture and geology, with changing related exhibits, forms the centerpiece of this 62-acre preserve covered by forest, thickets and meadows. There are about five miles of marked nature trails. Address: 50 Barry Drive, Glen Cove, NY 11542. Phone: 571-8010. When to visit: Museum open Tuesday to Saturday, 10 to 4; Sunday, 1 to 4; closed Mondays. Preserve open daily, 8:30 to dusk; closed Christmas and New Year's Day.

In the foreground is a herring gull (*Larus argentatus*), white, gray wings with black tips. Standing on the rock is a double-crested cormorant (*Phalacrocorax auritus*), black with yellow cheeks. The flying bird is a common tern (*Sterna hirundo*), white with gray wings and a black cap.

**Twin Lakes Preserve.** Numerous different trees and other plants can be observed in this preserve's woodlands, swamps and ponds—all magnets for wildlife. Address: Old Mill Road, Wantagh, NY 11793. Phone: 431-9200. When to visit: Monday to Sunday, dawn to dusk. Guided tours are available by arrangement.

A twelve-spot skimmer (*Libellula pulchella*)—head and thorax chocolate-brown, abdomen grayish-brown, brown spots on wings—hovers over the purplish flowers of pickerelweed (*Pontederia cordata*). Behind the plant are two specimens of the Eastern painted turtle (*Chrysemys picta picta*), shell chiefly olive-colored, yellow plastron (lower shell), yellow and red stripes on neck and legs.

9

**Tackapausha Museum and Preserve.** Named for the sachem of the Massapequa Indians who sold the land that is now the Town of Hempstead, these 80 acres feature deciduous wet woods of red maple and white oak, ponds, clearings covered with wildflowers and swampland on which can be found one of the last stands of Atlantic white cedar on Long Island. Address: Washington Avenue, Seaford, NY 11783. Phone: 571-7443.

When to visit preserve: daily, dawn to sunset (inquire for museum hours).

The belted kingfisher (*Ceryle alcyon*) is blue-gray with a whitish throat and belly; the female has a rust-colored belly band. The forget-me-not (*Myosotis scorpioides*) in the foreground has light blue flowers with gold centers.

**Tackapausha Museum and Preserve** (*continued*). Atlantic white cedars (*Chamaecyparis thyoides*), special pride of the preserve, with a detail of cones and leaves. The birds are black-capped chickadees (*Parus atricapillus*), which have white cheeks, a black throat and buff-colored sides.

**Planting Fields Arboretum.** A former Gold Coast estate of the W. R. Coe family, the property includes a restored 65-room Tudor-Revival mansion and 409 acres of lawns, specimen trees and two greenhouses: one displaying camellias and the other a variety of orchids, ferns and cacti. The property is listed on the National Register of Historic Places. Address: Planting Fields Road, Oyster Bay, NY 11771. Phone: 922-9201. When to visit: daily, 9 to 5; camellia greenhouse, 10 to 4; main greenhouse, 10 to 4:30. Coe Hall tours, April through September.

Orchids (*Miltonia* sp.) in a greenhouse herborium. The flowers are yellow with brown spots and white "lips."

**Theodore Roosevelt Sanctuary.** Founded in 1923 by W. Emlen Roosevelt, a cousin of the 26th president, this is the oldest National Audubon songbird sanctuary. Its hilly, wooded 12 acres have been specifically planted to attract a wide variety of birds. The Trailside Museum offers educational exhibits, live wildlife displays and an observation room for watching feeding birds. The Sanctuary conducts natural history programs for all ages and research on local bird populations. Address: 134 Cove Road, Oyster Bay, NY 11771. Phone: 922-3200. When to visit grounds: daily, 9 to 4:30.

The yellow warbler (*Dendroica petechia*) is a male, as shown by the distinct (red) streaks on its (yellow) underside; beak, wings and tip of tail are very dark. It is perched on a flowering dogwood (*Cornus florida*); the flowers are white. In the background is a woodland path with a pool and a landmark statue.

**John F. Kennedy Wildlife Sanctuary.** On these 500-plus acres of tidal marshlands are several viewing blinds and an observation tower (see illustration). Address: Tobay Beach, Massapequa, NY 11758. Phone: 797-4114. When to visit: summer, 4:30 P.M. to dark; winter, 8 A.M. to dark. Apply for permit (no charge) at: ℅ Town of Oyster Bay, Dept. of Parks, 977 Hicksville Road, Massapequa, NY 11758.

The male Northern harrier (*Circus cyaneus*) is grayish above and mostly white below, with black wing and tail tips. The bayberry (*Myrica* sp.) at the lower right has grayish-white fruit.

**Muttontown Preserve.** Pedestrian, ski and equestrian trails crisscross this 550-acre "living museum" that features glacially formed rolling hills, kettle-hole ponds, meadow, woodland and other North Shore characteristics. Address: Bill Patterson Nature Center, Muttontown Lane, East Norwich, NY 11732. Phone: 571-8500. When to visit: daily, 9:30 to 4:30.

A reddish-brown woodchuck (*Marmota monax*) is munching on a black-eyed Susan (*Rudbeckia hirta*), which has golden-yellow ray flowers and a cone of brown disk flowers at the center.

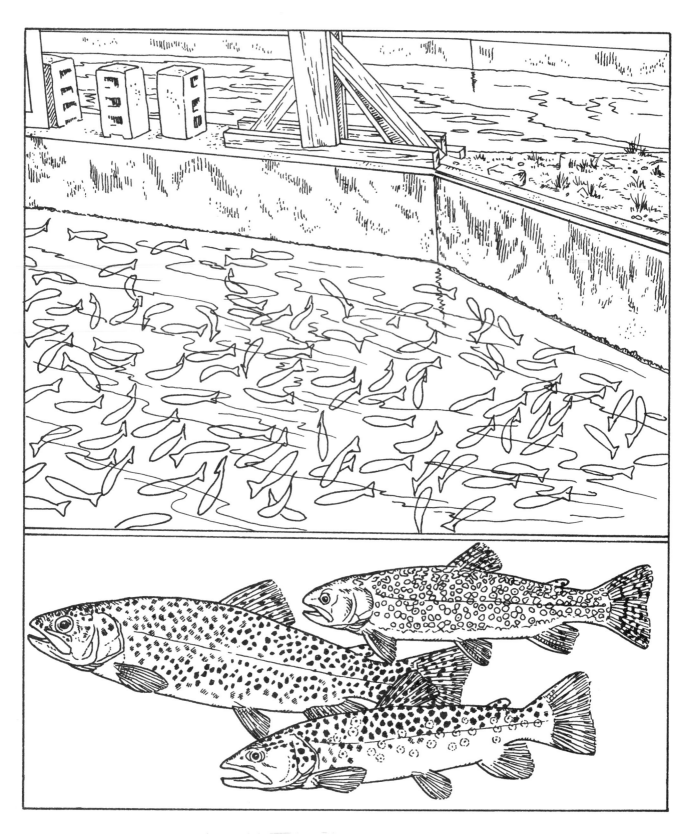

**Cold Spring Harbor Fish Hatchery & Aquarium.** This facility's 40 aquariums, outdoor rearing pools, indoor and outdoor turtle habitats and 20-foot indoor stream exhibition bring you eye to eye with New York freshwater reptiles, amphibians and fish. The Fairchild Building houses New York's largest collection of native amphibians. Address: Route 25A (on Nassau-Suffolk border), Cold Spring Harbor, NY. (Mailing address: P.O. Box 535, Cold Spring Harbor, NY 11724.)

Phone: 692-6768. When to visit: daily, 10 to 5; closed Thanksgiving and Christmas.

ABOVE: One of the outdoor ponds. BELOW, TOP TO BOTTOM: a rainbow trout (*Salmo gairdneri*), silvery blue with a pinkish streak down side, black spots on tail; a brown trout (*Salmo trutta*), brownish yellow with dark spots on sides; and a brook trout (*Salvelinus fontinalis*), olive-colored back, leading edge of bottom fins is white, followed by a black stripe.

**Cold Spring Harbor Fish Hatchery & Aquarium** (*continued*). One of the aquarium displays, featuring a spotted salamander (*Ambystoma maculatum*). Its belly is gray; above, it ranges from black to brown, with yellow or orange spots.

**Target Rock National Wildlife Refuge.** These 80 acres on Lloyd Neck peninsula consist of upland forest and rocky beach. The refuge supports a variety of birds, mammals, game fish, reptiles, trees and flowering plants. The "target rock," now isolated in the waters of Long Island Sound, is said to have been fired at for practice by British seamen in the Revolutionary War. Address: Target Rock Road, Lloyd Harbor, NY 11743. Phone: 286-0485. When to visit: daily, ½ hour before sunrise to ½ hour after sunset.

The upper bird is a (male) common yellowthroat (*Geothlypis trichas*): dark olive cap, back, wings and tail; black mask; yellow throat and breast. The lower bird is an American redstart (*Setophaga ruticilla*): glossy black, with orange patches mid-wing and upper tail. The birds are perched on a rhododendron (*Rhododendron* sp.); its flowers may be white, pink or purple.

**Target Rock National Wildlife Refuge** (*continued*). The bird species dominating this beach view (with Target Rock in the background) is the bank swallow (*Riparia riparia*), which is very dark, with white throat and belly.

**Uplands Farm Sanctuary.** This former dairy and sheep farm is now the headquarters of the Long Island Chapter of The Nature Conservancy. The grounds include fields, hedgerows, upland woods, farm buildings and a reference library. Address: Lawrence Hill Road, Cold Spring Harbor, NY 11724. Phone: 367-3225 or 367-3281. When to visit: Monday to Sunday, sunrise to sunset.

The foreground plant is a red clover (*Trifolium pratense*); the shade of red is magenta. The insects above are tawny-edged skippers (*Polites themistocles*); their wings are olive-brown with brighter tawny edges. The insect at the left is a (male) common sulphur butterfly (*Colias philodice*); its wings are light yellow with black borders.

20

**Caleb Smith State Park Preserve**. The Smiths, originally leasing from the Nesaquake Indians, lived on this land from 1663 into the 19th century, and the nature museum on the grounds was the original residence of Caleb Smith I. New York State purchased the land in 1963 and made it a nature preserve in 1989. The 543 acres include freshwater wetlands, ponds, streams, fields and upland woods. The Nissequogue River runs through the property. Address: Jericho Turnpike (east of Exit SM3), Smithtown, NY 11787. Phone: 265-1054. When to visit: 8 to 4:30; Tuesday to Sunday, April to September; Wednesday to Sunday, October to March.

In front of the museum house are several Canada geese (*Branta canadensis*): black neck and head, white "chin strap," dark wings, lighter underside.

**Hoyt Farm Nature Center**. This former estate, purchased from the Hoyt family by the Town of Smithtown in 1967, was the home of the Wicks family from the early 18th century (the main house dates from that century) until 1910. The 136 acres of wetlands, woodlands and cultivated lands also contain various specialized buildings, recreational facilities, a nature trail and a complex with live farm animals. Address: New Highway (east of Harned Road), Commack, NY 11725. Phone: 543-7804. When to visit: daily, 8 to dusk (separate times for Hoyt House and Nature Center).

Exotic chickens in front of a barn.

**Hoyt Farm Nature Center** (*continued*). Against a woodland background stands a wigwam in the style of the Delaware Indians, who once occupied western Long Island and the stretch of Atlantic seaboard down to the present state of Delaware.

**South Shore Nature Center**. This facility covers 206 acres of woods, ponds and marshlands and is home to many birds and such mammals as the white-tailed deer, red fox and muskrat. A variety of nature programs is offered. Address: Bayview Avenue, East Islip, NY 11730. Phone: 224-5436. When to visit: 9 to 5; April to October, daily; November to March, closed on weekends.

In the foreground are wood ducks (*Aix sponsa*). The male (on the log) is glossy green on top of the head and around the eye,

with some black on the "cheek" and back of the neck; throat white, breast burgundy with light spots, sides creamy, wings a mixture of brown, blue and red; tail green with burgundy beneath it. The female is mainly shades of brown with a white eyepatch and some blue on the wings. The ducklings are even plainer (browns and whites). Flying in the background are tree swallows (*Tachycineta bicolor*), dark greenish-blue above and white below.

24

**South Shore Nature Center** (*continued*). On a walkway through the swamp area are some raccoons (*Procyon lotor*), which are generally brownish except for the black areas and some white around the eyes and muzzle. The most conspicuous plant behind them is skunk cabbage (*Symplocarpus foetidus*).

**Bayard Cutting Arboretum.** This arboretum was begun in 1887 by William Bayard Cutting. The former residence contains a museum of natural history. The 690-acre grounds include wooded areas and a bog, with plantings of oak, pine, rhododendron and azalea. The arboretum's collection of fir, spruce, pine, cypress, hemlock, yew and other conifers is one of the most extensive on Long Island. Address: 466 Montauk Highway, Great River, NY 11739. Phone: 669-1000. When to visit: Wednesday to Sunday and holidays; May to October, 10 to 5; November to April, 10 to 4.

With the former residence in the background, a cabbage white butterfly (*Artogeia rapae*)—white with charcoal wingtips and spots—hovers beside a common foxglove (*Digitalis purpurea*), with purple flowers (sometimes pink or white).

26

**Bayard Cutting Arboretum** (*continued*). A mute swan
(*Cygnus olor*)—white with an orange bill—and its cygnets—
dingier in color—swim toward a clump of yellow flag (*Iris
pseudacorus*).

**Connetquot River State Park Preserve.** The diverse habitats—pine barrens, freshwater wetlands, mixed hardwood forests and oak-brush plains—of this 3400-acre park preserve located along the Connetquot River support a variety of plants and animals. Address: Sunrise Highway, Oakdale, NY 11769. Phone: 581-1005. When to visit: 8 to sunset; October to March, Wednesday through Sunday; April to September, Tuesday to Sunday. A (free) permit, required for casual access to the park, can be obtained by sending a letter with your name,

address, number of people accompanying you and reason for visiting.

Two white-tailed deer (*Odocoileus virginianus*)—reddish (summer) or grayish (winter) brown fur, white throat, underside and underside of tail—stand amongst thin white birches (*Betula papyrifera*). The flower at the lower left is pink lady's slipper (*Cypripedium acaule*): pink slipper-like lip petal veined in red, side petals greenish brown.

**Flax Pond Marine Laboratory.** This research and instructional facility, operated by the Marine Sciences Research Center of SUNY at Stony Brook, is located on Flax Pond, a 146-acre tidal wetlands preserve with an unmarked nature trail through the marsh. Address: 15 Shore Drive, Old Field, NY 11733.

Phone: 632-8709. When to visit: marsh, daily, dawn to dusk; lab, Monday to Friday, 8 to 5.

A male mud fiddler crab (*Uca pugnax*)—dark brown shell with lighter enlarged claw—has scurried out of its burrow in the tidal marsh.

**Fire Island National Seashore.** Fire Island National Seashore was established in 1964 to preserve the only developed barrier island in the United States without roads. Attractions include beaches, salt marshes, self-guiding nature walks, campsites and the Fire Island Lighthouse. Address of Park Headquarters: 120 Laurel St., Patchogue, NY 11772-3596. Phone: 289-4810. When to visit: The seashore is open year round; contact park headquarters for information on individual attractions.

A trio of piping plovers (*Charadrius melodus*)—sand colored above, white below with a dark band around the neck, yellow bill with black tip and yellow feet—pick their way through the surf, while a common tern (*Sterna hirundo*)—white with pale gray mantle and a black cap—hovers overhead.

**Merrill Lake Sanctuary.** Run by The Nature Conservancy, this sanctuary hosts a salt-marsh community with both low and high marsh zones. The sanctuary also serves as a nursery for fish and wildlife and is home to several nesting osprey. There is a self-guided trail. Address: Springs Fireplace Road, East Hampton, NY. Phone: 329-7689. When to visit: daily, sunrise to sunset.

An osprey (*Pandion haliaetus*) comes in for a landing on a fence post. This bird is blackish above and white underneath. It has a white head with a black cheek patch, and dark "wrist patches" on the lower side of its wings.

31

**Quogue Wildlife Refuge.** Nature trails in this 300-acre refuge encompassing the headwaters of Quantuck Creek reveal a wide variety of ecological habitats—ponds, swamp, freshwater bog, estuary and pine barrens. At the entrance to the refuge is the Distressed Wildlife Complex where incapacitated birds and animals are cared for until they can be released back into the wild. Address: Old Main Road and Old Country Road, Quogue, NY 11959. Phone: 653-4771. When to visit: daily, 9 to 5.

A spotted turtle (*Clemmys guttata*)—black shell with bright yellow spots—wends its way past arrowhead (*Sagittaria latifolia*), which has white flowers.

**Quogue Wildlife Refuge** (*continued*). Purplish-red Northern pitcher plants (*Sarracenia purpurea*) tower over fragile white starflowers (*Trientalis borealis*).

**Morton National Wildlife Refuge.** This refuge provides win-
tering, resting and nesting areas for waterfowl and protects
endangered and other wildlife. Located on a peninsula, the
187-acre refuge is fringed with beaches; upland forest, brackish
and freshwater ponds, a lagoon and open fields make up the rest
of the refuge. Address: Noyac Road, Sag Harbor, NY 11963.
Phone: 286-0485. When to visit: daily, ½ hour before sunrise
to ½ hour after sunset. Public access to the peninsula is prohib-
ited during the nesting season (April to August) to protect the
nest sites.

A red-tailed hawk (*Buteo jamaicensis*) perches on a fence post.
This bird has a grayish-brown back and wings, whitish breast
with broad bands of streaks across the belly; the upperside of
the tail is red.

**Morton National Wildlife Refuge** (*continued*). An Eastern chipmunk (*Tamias striatus*)—reddish brown with black, brown and white stripes—perches on the stump of a tree to watch a male common pheasant (*Phasianus colchicus*) strut by. This bird has a bronze body mottled with brown, black and green, a white neck ring and a glossy green to purplish head with red eye patches.

**Mashomack Preserve**. These over 2000 acres of oak woodlands, marshes, freshwater ponds, tidal creeks and coastline are administered by The Nature Conservancy. The preserve hosts ospreys, ibis, hummingbirds, muskrats, foxes, harbor seals, terrapins, rare plants, native orchids, lichens and ferns. Address: 79 South Ferry Road, Shelter Island, NY 11964. Phone: 749-1001. When to visit: Wednesday through Monday; 9 to 5, April to September, 9 to 4, October through March.

A hungry muskrat (*Ondatra zibethicus*)—reddish brown with light gray belly and black tail—eagerly gnaws on marsh grass.

**Mashomack Preserve** (*continued*). A pair of harbor seals
(*Phoca vitulina*) sun themselves amidst rocks and driftwood.
These seals can be dark gray with brown spots or dark brown
with gray spots.

**Riverhead Foundation for Marine Research and Preservation**. In addition to studying the marine environment, this organization also operates a stranding/rescue program for marine mammals and turtles and offers a variety of environmental education programs, including whale watch cruises. A new aquarium features fresh and saltwater animals from local waters. Address: 431 E. Main Street, Riverhead, NY 11901-2550. Phone: 369-9840. When to visit: Write for information on cruises and other programs.

Three humpback whales (*Megaptera novaeangliae*)—black back, white throat, chest and underside of flippers and tail—disport themselves in the waters off Montauk, watched by a shipful of eager whale watchers. In the background is the Montauk lighthouse. Above are herring gulls (*Larus argentatus*), white, gray wings with black tips.

# INDEX OF NATURE PRESERVES

# INDEX OF COMMON NAMES OF PLANTS AND ANIMALS

# INDEX OF SCIENTIFIC NAMES OF PLANTS AND ANIMALS